The Irish Potato Famine

The Story of Irish-American Immigration

GREAT JOURNEYS

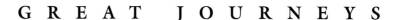

The Irish Potato Famine

The Story of Irish-American Immigration

by Edward F. Dolan

BENCHMARK BOOKS

MARSHALL CAVENDISH
NEW YORK

With many thanks to Professor Stephan Thernstrom of Harvard University for his careful review of this manuscript.

Benchmark Books
Marshall Cavendish
99 White Plains Road
Tarrytown, NY 10591-9001

Photo research by Candlepants Incorporated
Cover Photo: *The Emigrant Ship*, c.1880, Bradford Art Galleries and Museums, West Yorkshire, UK/The Bridgeman Art Library
The photographs in this book are used by permission and through the courtesy of:
The Granger Collection: 2–3, 13, 15, 18, 23, 28, 30, 34, 37, 42, 44, 47, 48, 58–59, 62, 64–65, 67, 70, 74, 76, 79, 80, 81, 97, 99; Culver Pictures: 8, 10, 26, 40, 50, 54–55, 87; Museum of the City of New York: 83, 94; Nevada State Historical Society: 84; New York Transit Museum Archives, Brooklyn: 85; Corbis: 93, 101, 102 (top); Corbis/Bettmann: 102 (lower).

Library of Congress Cataloging-in-Publication Data
Dolan, Edward F., 1924–
The Irish potato famine / by Edward F. Dolan
p.   cm. (Great journeys)
Includes bibliographical references and index.
Summary: Discusses the potato famine that devastated Ireland in the nineteenth century and led to a widespread immigration to the United States.
ISBN 0-7614-1323-5
1. Ireland—History—Famine, 1845–1852—Juvenile literature [1. Ireland—History—Famine, 1845–1852.] I. Title. II. Series.
DA950.7 .D65   2002   941.5081—dc21

Printed in the United States of America

1 3 5 6 4 2

Contents

Also by Edward F. Dolan

The American Revolution: How We Fought the War of Independence

Beyond the Frontier: The Story of the Trails West

Disaster 1906: The San Francisco Earthquake and Fire

Explorers of the Arctic and Antarctic

Jenner and the Miracle of Vaccine

Victory in Europe: The Fall of Hitler's Germany

Foreword

IN 1845, A DISASTROUS FAMINE STRUCK GREAT SECTIONS OF IRELAND. FOR the next six years, death and disease stalked the island country.

The tragedy was caused by the failure of Ireland's potato crop, a crop that had fed the nation's poorest people for centuries. The failure brought with it widespread starvation, the diseases that go hand-in-hand with major food shortages, the loss of hundreds of thousands of lives, and finally the desperate flight of people to survive and build new lives for themselves elsewhere in the world.

Their flight gave us one of the greatest journeys—and certainly one of the greatest adventure stories—in world history. In the six years that the famine took to run its course—from 1845 to 1851—more than a million men, women, and children fled their country. Risking their lives on long, storm-tossed voyages aboard overcrowded wooden ships, they sailed

This scene depicts women digging in a field in the fruitless hunt for the vanishing potato.

to Canada, Mexico, South America, Australia, New Zealand, and, in greatest number, to the United States.

Then, in the years that followed the famine, many Irish continued to leave their homeland and to settle elsewhere, especially in the United States, drawn by the advantages that the nation promised them.

Their journeys—not only during but ever since the famine years— have long stood as a testament to their courage and stamina. The same can be said of the years in their new lands. In those years, wherever the Irish have settled, they have established homes for themselves and their families; carved places in an ever-growing number of professions, trades, and arts; and participated in the political lives of the nations, serving in local, state, and national governments.

In the United States, they have joined with all the people who have come here from countries all over the world in search of new lives. Together, they have given the nation the diversity of views and backgrounds that is one of its greatest strengths and hallmarks.

A family looks at their ruined potato crop outside their cottage. Note the pigs and chickens behind the cottage. The animals provided food when all the family's potatoes had been eaten.

One

Famine

It was a disease that struck suddenly and silently in 1845. Ireland's potato crop had been perfectly healthy as it grew through the summer and approached its harvesting time that year. But then—in barely the span of a week—everything changed. It was a change that terrified the country's poorest people, the hundreds of thousands of peasant families who relied on the potato to keep them from starving. The potatoes in the ground and those in storage from last year's planting suddenly began to rot. The *Freeman's Journal*, a news magazine published in the city of Dublin, reported what was happening by telling the story of the farmer who ". . . had been digging potatoes—the finest he had ever seen—from a particular field . . . up to Monday last; and on digging in the same ridge on Tuesday he found the tubers blasted, and unfit for the use of man or beast."

Far more graphic was the report of a farmer's experience in western Ireland. This poor fellow "went out to the garden for potatoes for a meal. He stuck his spade in the pit (a shallow hole in which a peasant family stored its potatoes for daily use), and the spade was swallowed. His potatoes turned mud inside. He shrieked and shrieked. The whole town turned out."

The suddenness with which the blight struck and the agony that it brought were recorded by a traveling Capuchin priest, Father Theobald Matthew. In a letter to a friend in July 1845, Father Matthew wrote, "I passed from Dublin to Cork and this doomed plant bloomed in all the luxuriance of an abundant harvest. Returning [several days later], I beheld with sorrow one wide waste of putrefying vegetation. In many places the wretched people were sitting on fences of their decaying gardens, wringing their hands and wailing bitterly."

The terror and sorrow noted by the three writers was on hand everywhere that the terrible decay was seen. The remains of last year's potato crop suddenly turned rotten in the storage pits. Plantings that were to be harvested later in the year began to shrivel and die. Their flowers wilted and turned black. Inky spots appeared on the potatoes themselves, whether they were in the storage pits or still in the ground. The earth all around began to give off a sickening stench. It worsened as the days passed.

The farmers knew well what they were facing—a new onslaught of the mysterious disease called the potato blight. They also knew well the devastation that it brought whenever it struck. But all else about the disease was a mystery—its cause and the ways it progressed could not be fought. It was not until years later that agriculturalists learned it is triggered by a fungus called *phytophthora infestans* and can be successfully treated with copper-based fungicides.

But, in 1845, all that the Irish poor could say was that, once again, their land was facing the tragedy of famine, a shortage of food so severe

The entire peasant family lived in a single-room cottage with a floor made of hard-packed earth. The cooking fire was burned on the floor itself.

that it would lead to widespread starvation and sickness. Triggered by upheavals in the weather—either too much or too little rain, too much or too little heat—and by the human tragedy of war, famine had struck their island homeland at least ten times in the past five hundred years. It had claimed thousands of lives as it had deprived them of the various foods necessary for survival—grains, vegetables, and livestock. Now, suddenly, it had returned. It was to remain for six terrible years, ending finally in 1851.

The Potato and the Poor

This time, the potato was marked for destruction. The threat of its loss terrified the Irish poor. Over the centuries since its discovery by Spanish troops exploring the Andes Mountains of South America, the potato had made its way to all of Europe. By the 1840s, it had become a staple of Ireland's vast peasant class, a class that made up three-quarters of the people living in rural areas and three million of the entire population of just over eight million.

The peasantry survived by farming small patches of ground that they rented from the English, who had been the country's principal landowners since the twelfth century. The renters liked the potato because it could be planted quickly by placing its seeds in rows, covering them with dirt, and leaving them to take care of themselves. The farmer could then turn to other tasks to earn the money desperately needed for his family. With his fellow tenants, he could grow vegetables, wheat, corn, barley, and rye for sale to his British landlord, who would then sell them to Britain. Or he could do odd jobs for the landlord. Or sign aboard the fishing boats that ventured out into the Atlantic Ocean or the Irish Sea. At last, when harvest time came around, he could return home, dig up his tiny potato crop, and store it in the pit next to the family cottage. It could then be used daily, a few potatoes at a time, through the coming months.

The crop was vital to his family's survival. Over the centuries since its arrival, the potato had become the basic food of Ireland's poor. They ate potatoes three times a day, usually washing them down with skimmed milk, buttermilk, or tea. For many, it was their only food except for a few vegetable plantings and the doomed pig or cow that the family kept to carry them through those times when the last of their supply of potatoes ran out before a new crop could be harvested.

At one time, wheat, corn, barley, and rye had been mainstays in the Irish diet. But, starting in the 1600s, the potato had steadily replaced

Thousands of people left their homes to search for any food that was to be found. They carried with them a few household utensils, such as a kettle for heating water.

them on the tables of the poor because it could be grown so cheaply and with so little care. This was especially true of the gray, ugly, hard-to-digest potato called the lumper. It became the favorite of the poorest of the poor after being introduced into the country as feed for pigs.

The conditions that led to the widespread use of the potato among Ireland's poor had begun in the 1100s, when England's King Henry II had made himself overlord of Ireland. In the next centuries, the British had taken over most of the country's lands, with one of the most blatant land grabs occurring in the late 1600s. It was then that the British, principally a Protestant people, banned the Roman Catholic religion in Ireland. Wealthy Catholics were stripped of their homes and wealth. Many were gradually turned into paupers and joined the country's extensive poor class. The British then rented the lands back to the former owners (or their descendants) in small parcels of one to ten acres. The landlords exacted high rents and paid the tenants very low wages to raise crops and livestock on most of the rented land for export to England. Just enough space was left for the renters to have a small hut with a thatched roof for a home and enough ground to grow one crop for their families—the lowly potato.

Wheat, corn, barley, and rye continued to be harvested in Ireland in the mid-1800s, but they were beyond the means of the country's poor. They were harvested chiefly for export to England and for purchase by the wealthy classes—British and Irish alike—at home. In fact, three-quarters of the nation's usable land was devoted to corn alone.

When Famine Struck

The disease that killed the potato crop in 1845, historians believe, probably entered Ireland aboard a ship from America. The six years that it then remained on the scene were marked by starvation and disease and by a lack of rain (not only in Ireland but throughout Europe) that made matters worse. Lost in those years were the lives of about one million people. In addition, more than another one million men, women, and children fled the country, seeking new lives in England and Scotland, Australia, Canada, and, especially, the United States.

The living conditions of the poor when the famine struck were deplorable, just as they had been for centuries. At the time, Ireland was one of the most poverty-stricken nations in Europe. Uneducated and with little chance to better themselves, the poor seemed to have little ambition. Their attitude was widely thought to be the result of having been kept for so long under the thumb of their British masters. Over the first decades of the 1800s, their plight had been described by many visitors, among them a French writer named Gustave de Beaumont. "I have seen the Indian in his forests and the Negro in his chains, and thought, as I contemplated their pitiable condition that I saw the very extreme of human wretchedness, but I did not then know the condition of unfortunate Ireland," he wrote.

Reporting that he found the poorest of English paupers "better fed and clothed than the most prosperous of Irish laborers," de Beaumont wrote of seeing pigs and families sharing the same huts, and of meeting people in many areas who were dressed in rags and sickly from unhealthy living conditions.

The British government also recognized the plight of the Irish poor in the nineteenth century. Between 1800 and 1845, Parliament appointed 114 royal commissions and 61 special commissions to investigate the terrible living conditions of the poverty-stricken and to make recommendations for improvements.

One of the most important of the groups—called the Devon Commission—launched a study of the Irish peasantry in 1843 and issued a report of its findings two years later. In the report, the commission echoed de Beaumont's views, charging that "[i]t would be impossible adequately to describe the privations which they habitually and silently endure . . . [I]n

Everyone in the cottage, from young children to older adults, had to hunt for food during the famine, after the last of the family's potatoes and animals had been eaten.

many districts their only food is the potato, their only beverage water . . . Their cabins are seldom a protection against the weather . . . [A] bed or a blanket is a rare luxury . . . and nearly in all, their pig and a manure heap constitute their only property." The commission urged the British government to undertake a program that would turn nearly four million unused Irish acres into productive farmland. The government did not act on the recommendation.

Ironically, the ink was barely dry on the commission's report before the famine made its appearance. It came on the scene with a misleading slowness. In 1845, only about a third of the potato crop was lost, followed by a larger loss in 1846—three-quarters of the crop. The heaviest loss came in 1847, which earned the nickname Black '47.

Starvation and the tragedies that accompanied it—disease and death—swept through much of Ireland in those years. Hardest hit were eleven of the island country's thirty-two counties—Galway, Mayo, Sligo, and Roscommon in the west; Cork, Kerry, Limerick, and Tipperary in the south and southwest; and, in the north, Cavan, Fermanagh, and Monaghan. Out of the hunger there came such agonized cries as the verse written by an unknown poet and printed in an 1846 edition of *The Illustrated London News*:

> Alas! The foul and fatal blight
> Infecting Raleigh's grateful root,
> Blasting the fields of verdure bright
> That waves o'er Erin's favorite fruit.
> The peasant's cherished hope is gone,
> His little garden's pride is o'er,
> Famine and plague now scowl upon
> Hibernia's fair and fertile shore.

"Scowl upon" is too gentle a phrase to describe the effect of the

famine on the country. Hunger spread quickly and as it intensified families desperately tried to save what they could of their potatoes by peeling away the rotting sections, grating and boiling what remained, and making it into boxty bread (potato bread). That concoction brought on the first illnesses of the famine—potentially fatal stomach cramps and dysentery. Next, the people slaughtered their pigs and cows, and in the mountain areas, their sheep. When their animals were gone, they scoured the beaches for limpets (small shell snails that cling to rocks or timbers) and seaweed, and the countryside for whatever it could surrender—weeds, roots, nettles, flowers, and the remnants of animal feed—just as they had done in earlier famines. Their hunger was relentless. It worsened daily, bringing on a weakness that left them vulnerable to a host of silent horrors, among them scurvy, an eye ailment called xerophthalmia, cholera, typhus fever, and relapsing fever.

The poor, however, were not the only ones who fell prey to the horrors that stalked the country. Members of the middle and upper classes were also struck, especially by the highly contagious diseases. The victims were principally those whose occupations brought them in contact with the sick—physicians, clergymen, public employees, and deeply concerned private citizens who worked to supply the starving with food.

Hunger also affected the middle and upper classes. The flow of potatoes meant for sale to the general public ran dry when plague-ridden farmers did not have the strength to plant new crops. Thus, both the famine and the contagious diseases reached out to touch people of all classes, from the neediest to the wealthiest.

But the hardest hit remained the country's poorest. Thousands of tenant farmers and their families lost their cottages and bits of land when, too ill to plant crops for their landlords, they were no longer able to pay their rents. They now roamed the countryside in search of food and work. Their quest for survival often took them far from home and thus spread their diseases to new locales. The sick and starving

Silent Horrors of the Famine

Among the silent horrors of the famine years, two of the most dreaded were scurvy and xerophthalmia, both now known to be caused by a lack of two vitamins—vitamin C in the former and vitamin A in the latter. Victims of scurvy were plagued with bleeding gums, swollen and painful joints, and broken blood vessels that discolored the skin and caused the disease to be nick-named black leg scurvy. The victims of xeropthalmia were usually children under fifteen years of age. If untreated, it led to blindness, usually in one eye only.

Cholera is a bacterial infection that usually strikes its victims after they drink contaminated water. Its symptoms begin with diarrhea and, often, vomiting. Then come muscle cramps, an icy skin, and a severe thirst. If fluids and salt are not promptly replaced, coma and death often follow within twenty-four hours. Cholera is still a threat in India today. A vaccine made from dead cholera bacteria provides limited protection.

The greatest killer of all in the famine years was simply called "the fever." It was a contagious disease that had periodically appeared in Ireland for centuries. Actually, it was caused by two infectious diseases occurring simultaneously in the victim—typhus fever and relapsing fever. The two shared one characteristic in common—a raging body temperature. Typhus also featured prostration and mental confusion, while relapsing fever was marked by nausea, vomiting, and jaundice. Both frequently ended in death and both occurred most often in conditions that were marked by infestations of lice.

One of the most tragic sights throughout the famine years was of workers who removed the dead from ditches, fields, and roadsides for burial.

How were the famine and the two fevers connected? Starving and exhausted people were unable to clean their homes, their bedding, their cooking utensils, and themselves. A growing filth produced widespread infestations of lice and encouraged the spread of disease in the weakened population. Adding to these problems, the fevers—along with the other illnesses of the day—left the victims too weak to plant new crops of potatoes that might be healthy and thus hasten an end to the starvation.

crowded into what were called workhouses. These were public facilities that the British government had built over the years to provide beds for the ill and destitute. By early 1847, the workhouses were filled to capacity and were recording three thousand deaths a week. Death was to be seen everywhere. In 1846, an official with the city of Cork wrote of a horror he came upon when he entered a peasant hut:

> Six famished ghastly skeletons to all appearances dead were huddled in a corner on some filthy straw, their sole covering what seemed to be a ragged horse-cloth and their wretched legs hanging about, naked above the knees. I approached in horror and found by a low moaning that they were alive—they were in fever—four children, a woman and what had been a man.

Also writing in 1846 was author William Carleton. He saw sickness and death wherever he looked:

> The features of the people were gaunt, their eyes wild and hollow, their gait feeble and tottering. Pass through the fields, and you were met by little groups bearing home on their shoulders, and with difficulty, a coffin, or perhaps two of them. The roads were literally black with funerals, and as you passed from parish to parish, the deathbells were pealing forth in slow but gloomy tones the triumph which pestilence was achieving over the face of our beloved country—a country that was every day filled with darker desolation and deeper mourning.

In time, Ireland became a vast graveyard—a graveyard of pits where the dead were wrapped in sheets and covered over with dirt once the country's supply of caskets ran out. There they had to remain until full burial was possible. In the meantime, starving animals fed themselves on the corpses, and there were even some reports of cannibalism. Finally, a new type of casket appeared, a macabre one built especially for the times—a reusable model. It was equipped with a trapdoor that was triggered open in its floor when a corpse was being lowered into the grave. Then it was ready for further use.

Food in the Midst of Starvation

The famine was marked with an oddity that had been seen in earlier years of privation—the presence of ample food in the midst of terrible want. While the people starved, the landowners shipped tons of wheat, corn, oats, barley, and rye to Britain each year—enough wheat alone, claimed one observer, to have fed the entire Irish population.

Early on in the famine, however, the British government in London did take a step to help Ireland. In the autumn of 1854, seeing that the country was threatened with an impending famine, the authorities in London purchased tons of Indian corn and meal from the United States and had it stored in Irish warehouses so that it could be put on sale at extremely low prices when the shortage of food became too severe.

The idea was a good one, but it had a serious shortcoming. The Indian corn—which the Irish called brimstone for its yellow color—presented several unforeseen problems, the worst being that it was extremely hard and thus very difficult for most mills to grind thoroughly. It was also difficult to cook. In an 1854 issue of *Dublin University Magazine*, William Wilde, a physician, noted that "[t]he poor were totally unacquainted with the mode of preparing Indian meal for food; indeed, in many instances they ate [the meal] raw. Some had no fuel, others were too hungry to carry it home, and all were ignorant of . . . preparing it either as stirabout or bread." (Stirabout is a porridge made of cornmeal or oatmeal boiled in water and stirred.)

When poorly ground and improperly cooked, Indian meal raised havoc

Most Irish people suffered silently during the famine. Some, though, grew so angry that they attacked stores where a better grade of potato than the lumper was sold to upper-class families.

with those who ate it. The grain, hard and sharp-edged, was difficult to digest and could easily pierce the walls of the intestines. Fear of its dangers caused the Irish to shun the corn for the first years of the famine. Only when their hunger became too great did they dare to eat it despite the likely side effects.

Though the British government in London acted swiftly in securing the shipments of Indian corn and meal, it was slow to help the Irish in other matters. But, in 1847, it finally took two steps to ease their suffering. It established soup kitchens that supplied daily meals for the needy. It then launched a series of public works projects to provide the poor with employment.

Of the two steps, the soup kitchens proved to be the more valuable. They provided needed meals daily—usually consisting of a quart of soup thickened with meal, plus four ounces of bread or biscuit—for more than three million starving people; the meals were free and required only that the people bring their own bowls. Soon, the government kitchens were joined by others that were formed by the Society of Friends, a religious group, and a number of individuals and private organizations. As for the public works projects, they would have been comic had not the famine been producing so much tragedy.

Why? Because the British government dictated that the jobs done under the program must never take work away from private companies and their workers. Consequently, for a few pennies a day, Irish laborers in the program were set to building roads in rural areas where they were not needed; often, they went nowhere and ended abruptly in the middle of a field or a bog. On the other hand, projects that could have benefited the country were ignored—for example, the construction of railroads and the development of additional deep sea fishing boats and equipment. Both of those projects would have provided widespread employment when completed. Further, of course, the development of Ireland's fishing industry would have provided food for protection against future famines. But,

Ireland's wealthier people attempted to help the famine victims by opening soup kitchens to feed them, and, as shown in this picture, by distributing clothing to the needy.

designed as it was, the program was doomed. It was canceled within a few months, putting close to five hundred thousand people out of work.

"Silent" is the most appropriate word to describe the demeanor of the Irish poor during the first year of the famine. Silently, they watched their loved ones weaken and die, and then fell silently ill themselves. Silently, they watched the Irish grains and animals that could have saved their lives depart for English markets under armed guard.

During that first awful year, there was little or no talk among them of escaping to new lives elsewhere. But in 1846, the silence was suddenly broken by three developments. First, as the homeless took to the roads in search of work or food, the diseases of the famine began to spread far beyond the original eleven stricken counties. Second, the potato crop of 1846–1847, after promising to be healthy, suddenly blackened and turned as foul as before. And, finally, the winter crowned the year's agony by being one of the coldest and snowiest ever recorded in Ireland.

As a consequence, on a rising tide of horror, thousands of people—men, women, and children from all walks of life—began moving as one in that year. Terrified, they began to seek out the ships that could carry them away from their stricken homeland to distant nations across the world, especially the young United States.

Hoping to escape the famine, a businessman studies the boat fare to the United States. This painting appeared in an English magazine in 1854.

Two

Seeking a New Life

THE VERY FIRST JOURNEYS OUT OF THEIR HOMELAND BY THE IRISH WERE not made during the famine years. Rather, the earliest of the travelers dated back to the seventeenth century. In the fifty years before 1776, about 250,000 Irishmen and women departed west across the Atlantic. Most did not leave voluntarily, but were banished as criminals or rebels to work on the tobacco plantations of colonial America and the sugar plantations of the West Indies. Others, when unable to pay their debts, were sent west by the courts to work as indentured servants for families or businesses until their debts were cleared. The length of time served depended on the amount of money owed.

Next, in the 1700s, a few hardy souls, mainly Protestants, began venturing out to Canada and the thirteen neighboring American colonies. Then, in the years between 1825 and 1845, more than eight hundred thousand Irish, both Protestant and Catholic, moved to North America.

Two-thirds of their number at first settled in Canada, but quickly chose the United States as their preferred destination. They did so because the country offered them greater opportunities for work and because Canada presented two difficulties: it was bitterly cold for much of the year and many of its people spoke French rather than English.

Then the famine struck, driving more than a million people to abandon their country in the grim years between 1846 and 1851. Only a few fled in the opening year of the famine, 1845, because most of the people were reluctant to leave their loved ones and because many feared the loss of their Catholic faith if they settled in the United States, which was principally a Protestant country. But then, in 1846, the number of those leaving jumped to 106,000, with 212,000 following in 1847. The annual totals fell to 178,000 in 1848 and then rose to 212,000 in 1849; 209,000 in 1850; and 250,000 in 1851. By the close of 1851, the number of departed had reached 1,167,000 and the famine was passing. But the journeys to new homes would continue for the rest of the century. Of the Irish who sailed to Canada during the famine years, an estimated 200,000 then made their way south across the border to the United States.

In all, the United States drew the greatest number of immigrants. But the totals recorded by other countries were impressive. In the ten years ending in 1851, the Irish population in England, Wales, and Scotland ballooned by three hundred thousand. In fact, many more than that stopped there first, and then moved on to other destinations. A smaller number—especially those with sufficient funds for the long voyage and then the task of setting up housekeeping in a new, far-away country—made their way the thousands of miles to Australia.

The Ships

THE EXODUS TRANSFORMED BOTH THE BRITISH AND AMERICAN SHIPPING industries. Before the famine, ships had carried the adventurers to their homes in the spring and summer, sensibly taking advantage of the calmer seas and skies. But now there were so many eager customers that sailings were also scheduled for the autumn and winter, with passengers and crews taking their chances on storms, high winds, angry seas, and a vicious cold that littered the North Atlantic with icebergs and floes.

Mustered for the year-round business were ships of every description and size. Among them were aged British and Irish schooners and barques that had once worked the slave trade, transporting their human cargoes from Africa to the Americas and elsewhere until the British government put them out of business by abolishing the slave trade, partly in 1807 and then completely in 1833. Working alongside them were sleek American packet ships of more than one thousand tons that carried the more prosperous of the fleeing Irish. And seen everywhere were smaller ships, everything from ferries to cattle boats and coastal freighters. They mostly took passengers to Irish and English ports where larger vessels could be booked for the ocean voyages. Some, however, were outfitted with extra masts and canvas so that trips to Canada and the United States could be risked. In all, some five thousand sailing ships made their way across the Atlantic during the six famine years.

Most of their number attempted no more than one to three voyages. Many were too small for ocean travel. Most were crudely adapted for the work by having bunks nailed together two or three tiers high, in their holds, often where cargoes of slaves had once been quartered. Working aboard some were incompetent officers and men who would have been unlikely to find jobs in normal times. Others had crews that quickly lost their enthusiasm for the work when the passengers fell desperately ill at sea with the diseases of the famine.

Many—if not most—of the ships did double duty during the famine years. They carried human cargo westward in the bunks belowdecks. On arrival in Canada or the United States, the crews ripped out the bunks and replaced them with cargo for the return home. Finally, the

Those leaving Ireland really had no idea what they were going to, but they knew they were escaping almost certain starvation—and death. These emigrants to the new land are encouragd by the blessing of their priest.

cargo was taken off the ship at journey's end and the bunks were once again nailed together.

In the opening years of the exodus, the ships sailed from a string of Irish ports, both large and small. Among them were Dublin, Sligo, Galway, Belfast, Londonderry, Tralee, and Limerick. Later, Britain's chief ports—London, Liverpool, Southampton, and Glasgow—became the most popular embarkation points, with Liverpool emerging as the most popular of all. Of non-British ports, Germany's Bremen and France's Le Havre ranked as the most favored.

The Cost of Sailing

THE COST OF AN ATLANTIC SAILING TO A CANADIAN OR U.S. PORT VARIED among the shipping companies. In great part, it depended on the distance to be traveled. Two well-known shippers—J & J Cooke and William McCorkell—charged between twelve and fifteen dollars in American currency for a ticket from Londonderry in Ireland to Canada's Quebec and seventeen dollars fifteen cents for passage by steerage to New York City. Wealthier travelers could take a cabin aboard a packet ship for between sixty and seventy-five dollars.

(Today, the prices for the tickets to Canada or New York City would buy sandwiches and milkshakes for you and a friend at a chain restaurant. Were you to sail today aboard a cruise ship for a week or two, your cabin would range in price from several hundred to several thousand dollars.)

What did the passengers get for their money? What they bought was governed as the years passed by a growing body of British and American maritime law. For those traveling in steerage—the cheapest way possible—each received a bunk belowdecks, in the ship's cargo hold. The bunk measured six feet long by two feet wide (in the very first days of the rush westward, the bunks were just twenty inches wide).

Author Herman Melville once served with the crew aboard a passenger ship during the famine. When he recounted his adventures in his novel, *Redburn*, he described the bunks this way:

These bunks were rapidly knocked together with coarse planks. They looked more like dog-kennels than anything else; especially as the place was so gloomy and dark; no light coming down except through the fore and after hatchways, both of which were covered with little houses called "booby hatches."

In addition, each passenger was allowed no less than ten cubic feet for the storage of luggage. These and other provisions were specified on the ticket, including: "Water and provisions according to the annexed scale will be supplied by the ship as required by law, and also fires and suitable hearths for cooking." Water was to be doled out at the daily rate of six pints per passenger and was to be used for cooking, drinking, and washing. If problems with the weather or the ship threatened to delay the vessel's arrival at its destination, the ration was to be cut accordingly.

The food provided on board was just enough to keep the passengers from starving. Beginning in 1815, international law called for all emigrant ships of all nations to carry food for their travelers. British shippers turned a blind eye to the regulation and, until 1842, expected their customers to supply their own food. That year, however, the British government began insisting that food be provided by the ships, with its cost to be included in the price of passage. Weekly, each passenger was to receive seven pounds of flour, bread, biscuit, rice, oatmeal, or potatoes—an average of one pound per day. Added to that allotment by law in 1849 were twice weekly distributions of tea, sugar, and molasses. All other foods were to be provided by the passengers themselves.

Initially, the passengers received raw food. Later—in 1852, two

The people who boarded a stagecoach for the first step on their way to a new life were the lucky ones. They had enough money to pay the fare. Most travelers had to walk to the ports where they hoped to sail to a new life.

years after the famine ended—a change in English maritime law made it mandatory for all ships leaving British ports to carry cooked rather than raw food. The change was ordered because so many passengers had become too ill during the voyages to do their own cooking. Three years later, the requirement became U.S. law for all ships bound for America.

The specification on the ticket that the ship would provide "suitable hearths for cooking" was something of an exaggeration, even for people who had lived in stone huts. Some vessels provided one to two small kitchens for passenger use, but the "suitable hearths" usually referred to either of two stoves—brick-lined boxes that were placed outside at intervals along the deck, or large stoves that Herman Melville described in *Redburn*:

Upon the main hatches, which were well calked and covered with heavy tarpaulins, the "passengers' galley" was solidly lashed down . . . This galley was a large open stove, or iron range-made expressly for emigrant ships, wholly unprotected from the weather, and where along the emigrants are permitted to cook their food while at sea."

The stoves were used mostly at sunset when the sea was likely to be calm because of the changing water and air temperature. Their use was never permitted in rough weather. The ship's officers kept an anxious eye on them and wasted no time in ordering their fires doused if they seemed to pose the slightest danger. Usually assigned the role of extinguishing them was a young seaman, always called Jack in the Shrouds. The Jack scampered into the rigging and dumped a bucket of water on each blaze.

The ticket concluded with the requirement that "bedding and the utensils for eating and drinking must be provided by the passengers."

Affording the Price of Passage

THE IRISH PEOPLE WERE KNOWN TO BE AMONG THE POOREST IN THE world. How could they possibly afford the costs of a move across an ocean to a new home? The truth was that many had almost no money whatsoever for the trip. Still, they made their way to the port cities, all hoping to raise the fare through some kind of work. The slum areas of the port cities were soon crammed full of hopeful job seekers. Some never escaped to set foot on a ship.

And what of those who did escape? First, poor though most of the travelers were, many were not completely without means. Also, some were able to raise passage money by selling what little livestock and personal possessions they owned. And some had also managed to set aside small amounts of money through the years that they could now put to use.

Further, in common with the people of every nation who came to the United States to start life afresh, families would often pool their money to send one of its members—perhaps an older brother—to the new home. Then the newcomer, on finding employment, would mail money home a bit at a time to be used by the next relative who was able to sail west. This system had been used for years and was described by an Irish official in 1834, some six years before the onset of the famine: "The general routine of emigration established here is that in the first place the most enterprising of the family goes out; he then sends for one of his relations; and in this manner the whole family is brought out at successive intervals."

In what seemed an odd turn of events during the famine, an estimated fifty thousand travelers were given the money for their passage by their British landlords. This may seem to have been a sudden and strange generosity on the parts of the landlords, whose principal—if not sole—interest in their tenants had always been the raising of crops and the prompt payment of rents. But there was a logical reason for all of it. The economics

With their emotions ranging from sorrow at leaving home to hope for the future, these immigrants take their final look at Ireland before sailing into the Atlantic. All are hoping that their loved ones will soon join them in their new homeland.

of Irish farming were changing. More and more landowners were finding that greater profits were to be made by combining their lands so that fewer tenant farmers were needed to care for them. More acreage could then be used for crops—and greater profits soon reaped. The result: The landowners refused to renew the leases for the tenant farmers, burned their cottages to the ground so that they could never again be inhabited, and then, to be rid of the dispossessed workers, offered many of them financial help in leaving the country to settle elsewhere.

But not only the very poor fled Ireland. The famine and the frightening diseases that went with it touched the country's middle and upper classes—everyone from the doctors who tended the suddenly ill to the people who worked in the soup kitchens to the families that, living in the midst of death, feared for their lives—and put them all to flight. When they sold their properties, their businesses, and their personal possessions, they made an exceptionally prosperous class of travelers. In fact, the first sailings of 1845 were booked mostly by the wealthy. Some had been contemplating for years a move that would let them start life over again in happier circumstances.

Setting Sail

SHIPS SAILED DAILY FROM THE VARIOUS PORTS IN IRELAND AND ENGLAND. The same scenes were repeated everywhere: passengers living in jam-packed rooming houses, in gutters, or even in tents or packing crates—as they waited to board a ship or tried to raise the fare for passage. Then there were the would-be passengers thronging the docks and attempting to buy passage westward; gullible new arrivals too often being sold tickets for bunks already purchased many times over by others. That was a cruel racket that ended the hopes of a new life for many a traveler and finally led families already in North America to book passage for their relatives and then send them the tickets rather than the money for the trip.

Many landlords evicted their tenants so that the various small farms could be joined to make large ones. Shown here is a landlord with the papers necessary for eviction. An armed government officer stands beside him, ready to lend support if required.

Finally, there were the lucky ones—passengers bidding tearful farewells to friends and relatives. Stopping them at every step of the way to the ship were hucksters peddling last-minute goods—everything from bits of food to items ranging from extra blankets to such useless items of nautical equipment as telescopes and sextants. Eventually, having made it

Farewell to Skibbereen

The town of Skibbereen in southern Ireland is remembered for its especially great suffering during the famine—a suffering that inspired an unknown tenant farmer to pen the following verse:

Oh, father dear, I often hear you speak of Erin's Isle,
Her lofty scenes and valleys green, her mountains rude and wild,
They say it is a lovely land wherein a prince might dwell,
Oh, why did you abandon it? The reason to me tell.

Oh, son! I loved my native land with energy and pride,
Till a blight came o'er my crops—my sheep, my cattle died,
My rent and taxes were too high, I could not them redeem,
And that's the cruel reason that I left Skibbereen.

Oh, well do I remember the bleak December day,
The landlord and the sheriff came to drive us all away;
They set my roof on fire with their cursed English spleen,
And that's another reason that I left old Skibbereen.

Your mother, too, God rest her soul, fell on the snowy ground,
She fainted in her anguish seeing the desolation round,
She never rose, but passed away from life to mortal dream,
And found a quiet grave, my boy, in dear old Skibbereen.

And you were only two years old and feeble was your frame,
I could not leave you with my friends, you bore my father's name—
I wrapped you in my cotamore at the dead of night unseen,
I heaved a sigh and bade goodbye, to dear old Skibbereen.

All seems to be confusion as, in the final hours before sailing, the passengers drag or carry their possessions on board. Many are carrying not only their clothing, but food, cooking utensils, and precious mementos from home.

through, they would at last manage to drag their luggage aboard and struggle to find their bunks belowdecks.

In *Redburn*, Herman Melville described the "bustle and confusion" that continued on board:

Added to the ordinary clamor of the docks, was the hurrying to and fro of our five hundred emigrants, the last of whom, with their baggage, were now coming on board; the appearance of the cabin passengers, following porters with their trunks; the loud orders of the dock-masters, ordering the ships behind us to preserve their order of going out; the leave-takings, and good-byes, and God-bless-you's, between the emigrants and their friends; and the cheers of the surrounding ships.

Despite the crowds, the excitement, and the confusion, the scenes of departure were ones of sadness to many of the journalists who witnessed them. To one writer, as he reported in an 1846 issue of *The Irish Quarterly*, the drama at dockside was "melancholy, most melancholy . . . the specta-cle is one of sadness and foreboding. A long continuous procession . . . of men, women, and children, with their humble luggage who are hurrying to quit for ever their native land."

In the writer's eyes, the scene was more than simply melancholy. It was tragic. In it, he could see the strength of his country ebbing away: "It is not a departing crowd of paupers but unhappily an exodus of those who may be regarded as having constituted . . . the bone and sinew of the land; the farmers and comfortable tenantry, the young and strong, the hale and hearty, the pride and prime of our Nation!"

Watching the ship as it departed Liverpool, a reporter could see a blend of awe and sorrow in the passengers:

Unlettered and inexperienced, everything seemed dreamlike to their senses—the hauling of blocks and ropes, the cries of busy seamen as they heave around the capstan, the hoarse cries of the officers, the strange bustle below and aloft, the rise and expansions of the huge masses of canvas that wing their floating home . . . Here are women with swollen eyes, who have just parted with near and dear ones, perhaps never to meet again, and mothers seeking to hush their wailing babes. In one place sits an aged woman . . . listless and sad, scarcely conscious of the bustle and confusion around her.

These reporters saw and noted the grimness of the departures. On the other hand, though, an 1850 edition of the *London Morning Chronicle* caught the frenzy often on display when late-arriving passengers finally reached dockside just as their ship was pulling away:

Many had to toss their luggage aboard from the quay, or to clamber on board by the rigging. The men contrived to jump on board with comparative ease; but by the delayed women, of whom there were nearly a score, the feat was not accomplished without much screaming and hesitation. . . . Here and there, a woman becoming entangled . . . [and] might be heard imploring aid from the sailors or passengers above.

When the latecomers tossed their luggage aboard, it didn't always make it:

Many a package missed its mark and fell into the dock, where it was rescued and handed up by a man in a small boat who followed in the wake of the mighty ship. When at last the ship cleared the

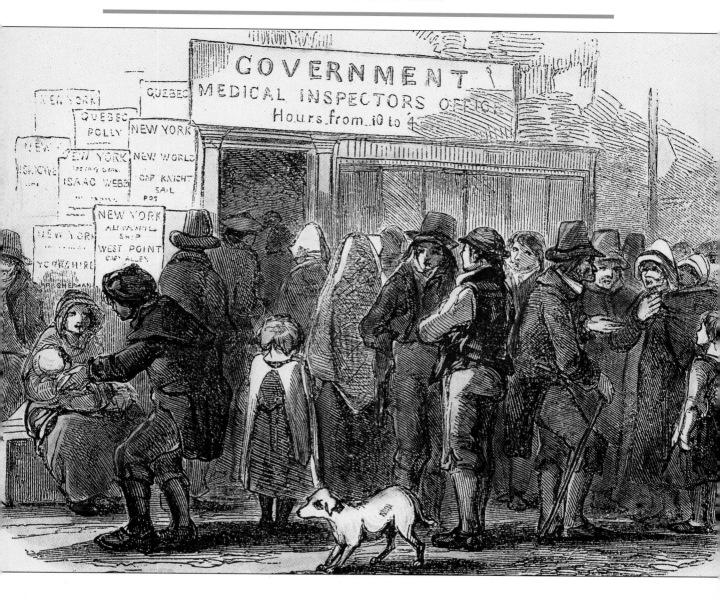

For the safety of their fellow passengers, many travelers had to undergo physical examinations to make sure they carried neither infectious nor fatal diseases on board. Failure to pass the examination meant failure to board. Many passengers were also examined on arrival at their destination, so that they would not carry contagious diseases to their new country.

Before a ship set sail, its crew searched the entire vessel for people who stole aboard because they could not afford the fare. When found, they were quickly, often roughly, put ashore.

gate . . . the spectators on shore took off their hats and cheered lustily, and the cheer was repeated by the whole body of emigrants on deck.

All the hope and wishes for a happy voyage that those cheers represented as they passed between ship and shore were soon replaced by the harsh realities of life aboard a ship too crowded, too storm tossed, and too laden with illness.

A brand new ship for the immigrant trade departs from the port of Cork on the Irish Sea. Named the Peru, *the vessel had space for 250 passengers.*

Three

On the Atlantic

THE ATLANTIC VOYAGE UNDER CANVAS TO THE UNITED STATES OR CANADA could be made in four to six weeks—if the weather permitted. But let a ship run into a storm, adverse winds, or the terrible absence of wind altogether and the voyage could stretch into months.

Herman Melville, again in *Redburn*, recalled how his ship, the *Highlander*, inched through three days of fog and rain after it left Liverpool. Then, when the weather cleared, the shout "Land ho!" echoed along the deck:

At the cry, the Irish emigrants came rushing up the hatchway, thinking America itself was at hand. "Where is it?" cried one of them, running out a little way on the bowsprit. "Is *that* it?"

"Aye, it doesn't look like *ould* Ireland, does it?" said Jackson.

Nothing could exceed the disappointment and grief of the emigrants when they were at last informed, that the land to the north was their own native island, which after leaving three or four weeks previous in a steamboat for Liverpool, was now close to them again; and that, after newly voyaging so many days . . . the *Highlander* was only bringing them in view of the original home whence they started.

They were the most simple people I had ever seen. They seemed to have no adequate idea of distances; and to them, America must have seemed a place just over the river. Every morning some of them came on deck, to see how much nearer we were; and one old man would stand for hours together, looking straight off from the bows, as if he expected to see New York City every minute, when, perhaps, we were yet two thousand miles distant.

The old man was one of the fortunate passengers. He was well enough to make his way outside, where he could breathe in fresh air. For all the steerage passengers, the space belowdecks was a prison at times— and often daily. Everyone was locked in when the hatches opening on the outer deck were tied down to keep the sea from crashing in during stormy weather. Many passengers remained imprisoned in their bunks for hours or days. Some, suffering one of the illnesses that raged back home, were too ill to move. Sometimes, their children were ill or restless and needed the comfort of being cradled in a mother's arms. Sometimes there was simply no place to sit or stand, so jammed were the spaces between the bunks with luggage and sacks of food that they had brought aboard in addition to the provisions that were supposed to be distributed by the ship. As the days passed the deck underfoot became filthy. It would not be washed down until the ship reached its destination.

Even when fresh air managed to enter the hold, it did little good. It was overwhelmed by the stench that was already there—the odors of air breathed too many times of unwashed, and, worse, diseased bodies; of rotting food; of vomit; and of death. When death occurred, the body was placed in a sack weighted down with coal and then hoisted to the deck outside. There, the passengers and crew gathered for a few moments of prayer before the body was lowered over the side and disappeared among the waves.

The foul air belowdecks produced one of Melville's most memorable sentences in *Redburn*: "We had not been at sea one week when to hold your nose down the forehatch was like holding it down a suddenly opened cesspool."

The foul air, though a major problem, was joined by others thought to be just as bad. Cooking, for one, was a nightly struggle, with the passengers, some green-faced with seasickness, inching their way up to the deck to light the stoves. There, they would wait in line to take turns to heat a piece of meat or several oatcakes that had been cooked back home so they would not spoil on the journey.

The nightly struggle almost invariably ended in the same way. The ship's captain, knowing the always present danger of fire on board, would watch the stoves constantly, and on sensing the slightest indication of trouble—anything from a sudden restlessness in the wind to an argument between passengers over who would cook next—he would order the flames doused. Dozens of hungry and disgruntled passengers were always left waiting with cold food.

The captain had a right to his fears. Fire was a constant threat aboard the wooden ships of the day and became a tragic reality on a number of occasions. One of the worst of those fires occurred without warning on the afternoon on August 24, 1848.

Dying Ships

LATE THAT AFTERNOON, THE AMERICAN PACKET SHIP, *OCEAN MONARCH*,

The crowded conditions that plagued the immigrant ships can be seen here. Many travelers—adults and children alike—became so sick from the rough sea and the foul air belowdecks that they could not leave their bunks for the entire voyage.

was cutting southwest through the Irish Sea, just a few hours after setting sail from England's Liverpool. Off to the starboard could be seen the coastal hills of Ireland. Crowding the ship's rail were its 364 passengers— 32 traveling first class and 332 in steerage belowdecks. With a mixture of sadness and anticipation, all were straining for a final glimpse of home before entering the Atlantic Ocean for the trip west to Boston.

Not one of their number had the slightest idea that a disaster was in the making. They knew only that they were traveling on a giant triple-deckered ship of thirteen hundred tons and that it had been launched just months ago for Boston's White Diamond Line. But there was disaster aboard, quietly taking shape in a passenger cabin at the stern—a growing haze of smoke and then, flashing suddenly, bursts of orange flame.

No one ever learned what caused the blaze. Among theories, the chief was that a seaman had lit a candle in a passage below the cabin while searching for possible stowaways and then had gone about his other duties, forgetting to extinguish it. Whatever the cause, the blaze had suddenly appeared and spread out of control within a few minutes.

When the blaze was reported by a steward, the ship's captain, James Murdoch, ordered the helmsman to head for the coast of Wales, just four miles off to port, and run aground there. But he saw within moments that his *Ocean Monarch* would never reach the shore before being engulfed in flames. The fire was spreading too rapidly. And so he ordered a turn into the wind and then sent two anchors plunging into the water, all in the hope of keeping the flames from spreading throughout the whole vessel.

But the maneuver was useless. Pandemonium erupted all along the deck. The crush of passengers at the rails, their struggle, and their screams and shouts—all the noise and furor made it impossible for the crewmen to hear the orders passed to them by Murdoch and his officers. In the confusion, the crew only managed to launch two lifeboats.

Fortunately, the *Ocean Monarch* was not alone in the Irish Sea that afternoon. Several ships—among them the American passenger ship *New World*, the British yacht *Queen of the Ocean*, and the Brazilian steam warship *Affonso*—were close by. They all hurried to the stricken vessel's aid. A passenger aboard one of these ships, Thomas Littledale, later provided a harrowing description of the blaze: "The flames were bursting with intense fury from the stern and center of the vessel. So great was the heat in these parts that the passengers, men, women, and children crowded to the forepart of the vessel. In their maddened despair women jumped overboard."

The Illustrated London News, in a late August edition, added the following to Thomas Littledale's description, reporting that many of the women hurled themselves "overboard with their offspring in their arms, and sunk to rise no more. Men followed their wives in a frenzy and were lost. Groups of men, women, and children also precipitated themselves into the water, in the vain hope of self-preservation. But the water closed over many of them forever."

When the passengers hurled themselves into the water, crewmen began throwing chairs, oars, luggage, and packing boxes—anything that would float—after them. Then into the water went the spars when, one after the other, the mizzen mast and the mainmast fell. (On a three-masted ship, the foremast stands closest to the bows. The mainmast comes next, with the mizzen mast located near the stern.)

Thomas Littledale recalled the scene:

There yet remained the foremast. As the fire was making its way to the fore part of the vessel, the passengers and crew, of course, crowded still further forward. To the jib boom they clung in clusters as thick as they could pack—even one lying over another. At length the foremast went boom, which, with its load of human beings, dropped into the water amidst the most heartrending

In one of the worst moments ever faced by travels, the Ocean Monarch *sank after burning along its entire length. This picture was copied from a drawing made at the scene by a passenger aboard a nearby ship.*

screams of both those on board and those who were falling into the water. Some of the poor creatures were enabled again to reach the vessel, others floated away on spars, but many met with a watery grave.

Small boats went plunging into the water from the ships that came rushing to the stricken *Monarch*'s side. Working their way as close to the flames as possible, they fetched passengers from the water, took them to safety, and then returned for others. Brazil's *Affonso* sent four ship's boats to the rescue and then swung a large paddlebox boat over the side. The *Affonso*'s officers and men rescued approximately 160 individuals, among them 13 crewmen. The *Queen of the Ocean*'s crew plucked 32 from the water.

Sinking slowly, the *Ocean Monarch* burned for twelve hours before disappearing beneath the surface. In the weeks that followed, 170 bodies were washed ashore, with many more never seen again. Only 203 passengers and 33 crewmen were saved. Among the surviving seamen was Captain James Murdoch. When the mizzen mast had come crashing down, he was forced to dive into the sea to avoid being crushed. He was later plucked from the water.

Of all the rescuers, one man was especially remembered for his heroism. He was Frederick Jerome, a seaman aboard the *New World*. As the ship's boat in which he was riding neared the flames, he dove into the water, swam to the dying ship, and climbed through a tangle of rigging to the deck and the terrified passengers still huddled there. He then lowered them, one at a time, to the waiting boat. Only when he had made certain that the last of their number had been removed did he join them for the return to the *New World*.

For his heroic actions, Jerome received a cash gift from Britain's Queen Victoria and was officially honored by the city of New York on his return to America. Jerome had been in the United States for only a short while before sailing on the *New World*. He had emigrated there from Portsmouth in England.

The *Caleb Grimshaw* took far longer than the *Ocean Monarch* to burn and sink. That ship caught fire with 425 passengers aboard while en route from England to New York in 1849. The burning vessel remained afloat for ten days before finally sinking. Tied to her during that time— and loaded to capacity with passengers—were two ship's boats and two rafts. With no further room aboard the boats and rafts, more than two hundred other passengers were still trapped aboard the ship itself as it struggled back toward the coast of Europe, hoping to be rescued. Help finally came in the form of the barque *Sarah*, bound for the Canadian port of Halifax from London. Only after everyone had been removed from the lifeboats, rafts, and the ship itself did the *Caleb Grimshaw* sink from sight. But ninety passengers had lost their lives in the ten-day ordeal.

A Frozen Terror

IN THE COLD TIMES OF THE YEAR, ANOTHER DANGER TO SHIPPING SUR-passed even the dangers of fire. It was the threat of collision with icebergs. In 1849 alone, four doomed ships crashed into the floating mountains of ice and sank. One of the greatest losses came in late April that year. The victim was the brig *Hannah*, with two hundred Irish emigrants aboard on a voyage to Canada.

At four o'clock in the morning, while approaching the Canadian coast, the ship blindly crashed into the foot of an iceberg and ripped open its hull at the bows. The captain—along with his first and second mates—swiftly freed a lifeboat and escaped into the dark, thinking that the ship was going to capsize in minutes. Left behind were the rest of the crew and all the passengers. The passengers, jarred awake by the crash and stunned to find seawater rushing through the ship, panicked. *The Illustrated London News* later reported that: "Their screams for help rent the air and it was with difficulty that the remainder of the crew could induce the frantic creatures to comprehend the only chance left of saving their lives. Fortunately, the ice was firm under the ship's bow and the seamen convincing them as to its security, many got on it."

Then, when the bulk of the passengers saw the firmness of the ice, they rushed madly to leave the ship: "Men, women and children, with nothing on but their night attire, went scrambling over the mass of ice. Many of the poor creatures slipped between the huge masses (of broken ice) and were either crushed to death or met with a watery grave. The last to leave the wreck were some of the crew, who contrived to save a small portion of spirits and a few blankets."

The death of the *Hannah* followed quickly: "Soon after they had got

Many ships brought the passengers up on deck every morning for a roll call of their names. The purpose was to find out if any of their number were too ill to leave their bunks or had died in the night. Illness was an enormous problem on the long voyages. The dead were removed for burial at sea.

clear, the ship's stern rose at it were above the water and she went down head foremost just 40 minutes after the collision with the ice."

Then the seamen "humanely gave up what covering they had to the women, some of whom had been shockingly wounded and bruised. Thus were they exposed to the whole of that day until five o'clock in the afternoon, when a vessel hove in sight and bore down on the edge of the field of ice."

The arrival, commanded by a Captain Marshall, was the Quebec-bound barque *Nicaragua*. Under his direction, the vessel inched up to the ice and began to remove the people there to safety: "The whole were saved. The number got on board the *Nicaragua* were 129 passengers and seamen, the greater part of whom were frost-bitten. As far as Captain Marshall could ascertain from the survivors, the number that perished by being crushed to death between the ice and being frozen to death, were between 50 and 60."

In the next days, many of the passengers were transferred at sea to other ships for the remainder of their journey westward. The *Hannah*'s skipper and the two men who had fled the ship with him were picked up at sea four days later. No word has been left to us of whether the three were punished for their desertion.

The Dreaded Diseases

DREADED EVEN MORE THAN FIRE AND SHIPWRECK WERE THE DISEASES THAT made their silent way among the travelers. Shipwreck took hundreds of lives, yes, but the diseases of the day took thousands.

Ranking high among their number were cholera, typhus fever, and relapsing fever. All three were suspected of being caused by the filthy conditions in which the steerage passengers lived. This, we know today, was not the case. The diseases were brought on board by people who were infected before they sailed.

Today, Asiatic cholera is known to be an intestinal microbe that is contracted through drinking contaminated water. It would be carried aboard while it was incubating in its victims and then, when the period of incubation ended, it would break out in all its fury.

Cholera began appearing on immigrant ships in the pre-famine days of the early 1830s. It returned in the famine years, first in 1847 and then in 1853. As frightful as cholera was, typhus was even more terrifying. Called "ship's fever," it had been a menace for centuries. In the famine years, it struck with its greatest fury in 1847, when it took the lives of about seven thousand sea travelers, most of them Irish.

Typhus, which most often occurred where lice were found, was known to develop best in filthy and overcrowded living conditions. The greatest number of deaths occurred among the travelers bound for Canada because the Canadian shipping lines charged less for passage than did their American competitors. Thus, Canadian ships drew the poorest of the travelers. In addition, the United States in 1847 inaugurated a number of measures that discouraged the poor from seeking passage on its ships and thus sent them shopping among the Canadian lines.

Though the worst of the illnesses, cholera and typhus were far from being the only health threats, travelers were also exposed to smallpox, dysentery, malnutrition, seasickness, infestations of body lice, and an ailment called rotten throat, which was possibly a strep infection. Most illnesses at sea struck in 1847. The death rate aboard the ships often hovered around 15 percent, but it mounted to 40 percent in some vessels

The newcomers to the United States are shown coming ashore at New York City in this 1858 engraving.

during the grim year of 1847. It earned the ships the frightening nickname, coffin ships.

A grim picture of what disease could do aboard a stricken vessel is

Years of Shipwreck

To speak only of the shipwrecks that occurred during the famine years is to tell just part of the story of the dangers that threatened the Irish as they sailed off to new lives. Those dangers were present to anyone who sailed the Atlantic Ocean both before and after the famine years.

For example, the winter of 1834—some eleven years before the famine—has long ranked as one of the most dangerous seasons ever faced by the emigrants. In that year, its stormy weather sent no fewer than seventeen ships to the bottom of the Gulf of St. Lawrence, off the coast of Canada, and 731 travelers were drowned.

Then, in 1852—the year following the end of the famine—fifty-one passengers died when the liner *St. George* caught fire in mid-Atlantic waters. Their deaths came on Christmas Eve.

What is remembered as the worst disaster of the era occurred in September 1858, when fire erupted on the iron steamship *Austria* while en route to the United States. Owned by the Hamburg-Amerika line, the vessel caught fire when hot tar accidentally exploded in flames while being used to air out the steerage area. Of the ship's 567 passengers, 500 were lost.

The destruction of the *Austria* may have been the worst of the nineteenth-century tragedies but the sinking of the *William Brown* was the most scandalous. It was lost on the night of May 19, 1841, when it crashed into a North Atlantic iceberg while sailing from England to Philadelphia.

The ship sank quickly, taking thirty of its sixty passengers with it. The

Aside from illnesses and fires on board, the dangers of the sea, not least of which were collisions with other oceangoing vessels, made it impossible for emigrants to be sure that they would ever see their new lands.

remaining passengers and all the crew escaped aboard two ship's boats. Into one went the vessel's captain, seven crewmen, and a woman passenger. It struck out for the distant Canadian coast and was never seen again.

It was the second ship's boat that turned the *William Brown* disaster into a worldwide scandal. Carrying first mate Alexander Holmes, eight seamen, and thirty-three passengers, it was pitching wildly in the sea and was in danger of being swamped. Such was the danger that Holmes ordered the crewmen to lighten its load by dumping six passengers overboard. The six were too numbed by the cold and too shocked by the ship's loss to resist the seamen who grabbed and manhandled them over the side.

But the sailors ran into trouble when Holmes, seeing water still crashing on board, ordered the death of a seventh passenger, Frank Carr. Carr frantically bargained for his life—as did his two sisters—but all for nothing. He was flung overboard and was followed in a moment by his sisters.

The ship's boat then survived the night. The next day, it came upon a passing ship, the eastbound *Crescent*. Holmes and his fellow survivors were taken aboard and carried to the French port of Le Havre. From there, the news of what had happened that night spread to a shocked world. Holmes was put on trial, judged guilty of manslaughter, and imprisoned for a number of years.

In 1937, some ninety-six years later, a motion picture based on the *William Brown* disaster was released. Titled *Souls at Sea*, it can still be seen from time to time on television today.

While shipwreck and fire at sea were always threats and while both did much damage, they were not disasters that were seen daily. A parliamentary survey of British ports during the five years between 1848 and 1853 revealed that, of the 6,877 ships that departed in those years, only 43 sank. Of the 1,421,704 passengers who departed in the same period, just 1,042 lost their lives due to fire or shipwreck.

provided by Herman Melville. In *Redburn*, he described entering his ship's hold after it had been sealed for several days due to "a malignant fever":

The sight that greeted us, upon entering, was wretched indeed. It was like entering a jail. From the rows of rude bunks, hundreds of meager, begrimed faces were turned upon us: while seated upon the chests, were scores of unshaven men, smoking tea leaves, and creating a suffocating vapor.

But:

This vapor was better than the native air of the place, which . . . was foetid in the extreme. In every corner, the females were huddled together, weeping and lamenting; children were asking bread from their mothers, who had none to give; and old men, seated upon the floor, were leaning back . . . with closed eyes and fetching their breath with a gasp.

Troubled by hardship and tragedy every step of the way, the famine ships at last struggled into port. There, whether in the United States or Canada, a new life awaited the Irish—one that would be marked by hardship but that would eventually become one of triumph for countless of their number.

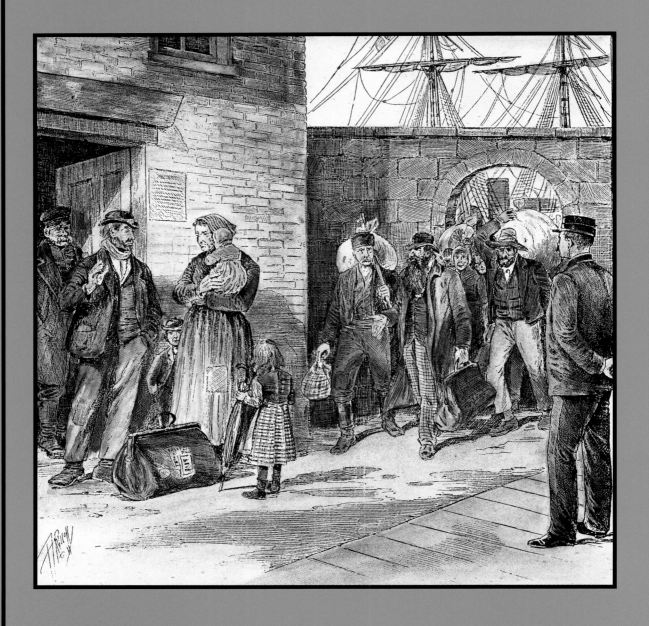

Many of the Irish who arrived in New York City in the mid-1800s went ashore at Castle Garden, which was to become the landing place for most immigrants until 1924. There, they were given temporary lodgings and their money was converted to American currency.

Four

A New Land, a Fresh Start

AS SOON AS AN IMMIGRANT SHIP DOCKED AT AN AMERICAN OR A CANADIAN port, medical personnel came aboard to check the health of the passengers. By now, the area belowdecks had usually been swept or mopped to save the shipping company the embarrassment of seeming careless of the vessel's appearance. Except for those too ill to leave their bunks, the passengers stood silently by, impatient to be free, frightened that they or their loved ones would be delayed because of ill health.

Early in the mass flight, both Canada and the United States established hospitals to care for the arrivals too ill to travel farther. In 1847, Canada designated Grosse Isle in the St. Lawrence River to be the nation's place for landing and, if necessary, hospitalizing its immigrants (Partridge Island off St. John, New Brunswick, also was used to receive and quarantine newcomers). That same year, the New York legislature called for the establishment of an immigrant hospital in New York City.

Of the two facilities, Grosse Isle dealt with far more cases of disease than did its American counterpart. This was because the United States, in 1846, imposed extremely strict health regulations that reduced the number of newcomers accepted by the country. The United States also cut the number of passengers allowed on its ships, decreeing that only two travelers would be permitted aboard for every five tons of a ship's registered tonnage. This meant that American ships could carry far fewer people than their British competitor, who was allowed three passengers per five tons of registered tonnage. As a result, the U.S. lines were forced to raise their prices if they hoped to show a profit. A growing number of travelers then began opting for the less expensive British ships.

Grosse Isle, a chunk of land approximately three miles long by a mile wide, lies some thirty miles east of Quebec. It had served as a quarantine station for immigrants suffering from cholera during an epidemic in the 1830s. Then it was destined for tragedy when it was designated a health center for new arrivals in 1847 and 1848. Both years were marked by typhus epidemics that began in Europe and then—joined by cholera, scarlet fever, and dysentery—spread westward aboard the crowded famine ships.

More than five thousand Irish arrivals died in those years while confined to Grosse Isle's fifty-bed hospital and the sheds and tents that were erected especially for the flood of patients. The actual number of deaths is known to have been much greater—perhaps as great as a harrowing fifteen thousand. Added to that overall total were the deaths that were recorded in the areas of Montreal and Quebec—the deaths of victims who showed the signs of their illnesses only after making their way past Grosse Isle.

Among the Grosse Isle dead were forty-four medical personnel. Lost as they worked among the sick were four doctors, twenty-two nurses and orderlies, six clergymen (four Catholics and two Protestants), three stewards, three police officers, and six workers who hauled supplies and buried the dead.

The United States fared well in the two epidemic years because of the stringent health regulations it established in 1846. In 1847, even as Grosse Isle became a sprawling graveyard, Boston escaped typhus altogether and New York suffered just 1,400 deaths out of thousands of arrivals.

Years later, in 1909, the Ancient Order of Hibernians in America unveiled a monument of gray stone dedicated to the memory of the Grosse Isle dead. The monument bears three inscriptions—in Gaelic, English, and French—carved on panels made of ebony. Each panel contains the same thought and reflects the same aura of tragedy, though each bears a slightly different wording. The English version reads: "To the sacred memory of thousands of Irish immigrants, who, to preserve the faith, suffered hunger and exile in 1847–1848 and stricken with fever ended here their sorrowful pilgrimage."

Coming Ashore

MANY—IF NOT MOST—OF THE IRISH WHO CAME ASHORE IN CANADA THEN made their way south to various locations in the United States. In pre-famine years, many Irish immigrants went, not only to New York City, but to Philadelphia and New Orleans. But, by the 1840s, most arriving ships were docking at the Battery, which was located at the southern tip of Manhattan Island in New York City. There, medical personnel would come aboard, check the health of the passengers, and clear for debarkation those found to be fit.

The ships were supposed to have their passenger lists ready for the immigration authorities. But, at times, there were so many vessels at dockside—and so many waiting to land—that there were too many customers for the medical staff to handle. The passengers who were fit enough to stand simply walked down the gangplank to their new lives, often carrying diseases that would erupt hours or days later.

Soon after arriving in the United States, many immigrants made their way to railroad stations for another great journey—this one to take them to live with relatives who had settled in various parts of the country.

For many, their first moments ashore would remain in their minds as the strangest in their lives. They were immediately accosted by salesmen trying to fast-talk them into buying railroad tickets to various locations; often, the tickets were fake. Joining the sellers were "runners," young men who grabbed the new arrivals' luggage and then led them away to check in at hotels and boardinghouses whether or not they wanted to.

One young workman recalled how he was accosted by two competing runners. One grabbed his suitcase, the other snatched his box of tools, with both then dashing off in different directions, leaving the young man staring after them with gaping mouth. It took him but a moment to decide what he must do. Since his livelihood depended on his tools, he instantly dashed after them.

At the time of his arrival, New York City was still trying to establish a landing depot for the Irish newcomers. The city had to wait until 1855—five years after the famine had ended but not the mass movement that it had inspired—for the depot to come into being. Called Castle Garden, it was located in a former theater on a small island off the southern tip of Manhattan Island.

It then became the major landing place for U.S. arrivals. Of all the different nationalities that flowed through its gates to new lives, more than two million were from Ireland. During their stay there, they received information about jobs, lodgings, and the costs of traveling to join distant relatives. Volunteer workers helped them write letters home and read job advertisements. On being cleared for release, they simply walked across a bridge to Manhattan Island and a new life.

The facility was described by Father Stephen Byrne, a Catholic priest, in a book of advice that he wrote for anyone planning a move to the United States:

All immigrants are obliged to land at Castle Garden, where they are provided with temporary accommodations suitable to their

Many of the new arrivals were forced to live in the worst, most dangerous neighborhoods, where rents were cheapest. Among the very lowest was the Five Points district in New York City.

requirements. Those who have tickets for the interior, or money to take them to any point outside of New York, are immediately put upon one or other of the great railroad lines diverging from the city to all parts of the country, without any trouble or risk to the immigrant . . . any immigrants having gold, silver, or uncurrent money of any kind can have it changed into current money of the United States, also at Castle Garden.

Castle Garden remained in business for thirty-five years, serving 70 percent of all newcomers to the United States. It was finally closed in 1890 and replaced by Ellis Island because it was no longer large enough to process all the people seeking entry into the United States.

Settling into a New Life

MANY OF THE EARLIEST IRISH ARRIVALS DID NOT VENTURE FAR FROM THE points where they had first come ashore. They chose nearby neighborhoods where their countrymen had settled before them—Five Points in New York City; Kensington and Moyamensing in Philadelphia; Irish Channel in New Orleans; and North End in Boston. All were older districts where enterprising landlords took full advantage of the influx by converting all the buildings in sight—warehouses, offices, private homes, and even the mansions of a bygone day—into living quarters for the flood of arrivals. Even backyards and alleys were not spared; they too were soon crowded with tiny shanties. Without proper sanitary facilities—or any at all—and with gutters and walkways littered with trash, all these areas were transformed into slums overnight, festering with the illnesses that many of the newcomers had brought with them and with new diseases generated in the neighborhoods themselves.

The crowded, suffocating conditions caused an English writer to

Ellis Island

On January 1, 1892, a fifteen-year-old Irish girl from County Cork arrived in upper New York Bay aboard the steamship *Nevada*. Her name was Annie Moore and, when she stepped ashore, she became the first person to enter the new U.S. immigration station at Ellis Island. Following at her heels were her two younger brothers. All three were on their way to live with their parents in New York City.

For the honor of being the first arrival at Ellis Island, Annie was personally welcomed by an immigration official and received a ten-dollar gold piece as a souvenir. The island of twenty-four acres was just a short distance off the New Jersey coast, and served as the chief immigration station for the United States until 1943, a total of fifty-one years.

During that half-century, more than one million Irish men, women, and children passed through Ellis Island. They were joined by a mounting flood of immigrants from various points in the world. In the busy years between 1895 and 1924, twelve million newcomers made their way through the island.

The island was named for its owner in the late 1700s—Samuel Ellis. It passed into the hands of New York State and then was purchased in 1808 by the U.S. government for use as a fort and an arsenal. It became an immigration station when Castle Garden was finally unable to handle the ever-mounting flood of immigrants.

On arrival, all newcomers were given a battery of physical and mental tests. If found physically and mentally fit, they were issued a health inspection

Life was no better than it had been back home for many of the immigrants. Seen here are desperately hungry families searching for food in a New York City garbage dump.

card, which was required for entry into the United States. If deemed unfit, they were returned home so that they would not became wards of the government.

Though Ellis Island ended its service as an immigration center in 1943, it continued to function as a detention facility for immigrants until 1954. Since 1965, it has been a part of the Statue of Liberty National Monument.

remark: "The great bulk of the Irish have blocked up the channels of immigration at the entrance and remain like the sand which lies at the bar of a river mouth."

Why did so many of the newcomers remain so close to the spots where they had first stepped ashore? The question has two answers. First, many did not have the money to travel farther. They had to stay put in the hope that they could work and eventually save enough for a move. It was a hope that never materialized for many. Second, though they had been willing to challenge the Atlantic Ocean, many were not willing

The places where countless newcomers had to live were no better than their cottages back home. Proof of that is seen in the grim interior of this New York City tenement.

to travel deep into a country whose lands and people were unfamiliar to them. These people preferred to remain with their own kind.

Still, the Irish who had traveled to North America in the 1700s had ventured out to the frontier and had made a success of farming in Pennsylvania, the Cumberland Valley, Virginia, and the Carolinas. But the newcomers did not have the funds to travel to the U.S. interior nor to buy farms for themselves, and they were completely untrained for a life in American agriculture. After years of tending to tiny potato plots and the small holdings of their landlords, they did not know how to till,

The least fortunate of the new arrivals were those who could not afford lodgings at all. They spent their nights in any spot where they could lie down to sleep, such as the basement floor of this New York police station.

plant, or harvest farm sites that spread themselves over hundreds of acres.

Still, many of the newcomers *were* willing to travel. They looked everywhere for work and took on any kind of job they could find, no matter how backbreaking and demeaning it might be. Even when employed, their lives were hard. Many were hated by their employers and supervisors because of their religious beliefs. Their lot in life was summed up in a letter written by a highly literate railroad worker in the American South:

It would take more than a mere letter to tell you of the despicable, humiliating, slavish life of an Irish worker on a railroad in the States; I believe I can come very near it by saying that everything, good and bad, black and white, is against him; no life for him— no protection in life; can be shot down, run through, kicked, cuffed, spat upon.

But, despite their troubles, many wrote glowing—and quite false— reports of how they were faring, as was pointed out in an 1848 letter William Dever sent to his family in Ireland:

Many write home that they are happy and wealthy . . . I heard friends of a young man in this city enquiring if [he] was not a banker here, as he wrote home that he was and persuaded all his relatives to come join him. But what was he, think you? He was sweeper of the office of the bank. They were astonished when told so. And thousands are just like him.

Indeed, they were. The men worked in mills, factories, mines, and sewers; they dug ditches and shoveled up the droppings of horses from city streets; they joined work gangs that built everything from homes to factories and dams, laid down city streets, and installed lighting systems.

Young Irishmen gather in an Irish neighborhood called Mullen's Alley. As did other races that came to the United States, the Irish preferred to gather together in their own neighborhoods.

One of the most difficult jobs available in the United States was mining. Mines in Pennsylvania, Nevada, and Montana provided ready—but hazardous and often tragic—employment for thousands of Irishmen. Accidents and harsh working conditions were common.

In all, they helped to build the United States that took shape from the Atlantic to Pacific coast in the 1800s and dawning 1900s, usually working for no more than a dollar a day.

From their earliest days in the United States, the Irish served as laborers on some of the country's major construction projects—the Erie Canal (opened in 1825), the Erie Railroad (opened in 1851), the nation's first transcontinental railroad (the final spike was driven at Promontory

Irish laborers are seen at work during the 1904 construction of streetcar tracks in New York City.

Point, Utah, in 1869), and the Statue of Liberty (completed in 1886).

The men were not alone. The women joined them, working in textile mills, sewing clothing in sweat shops, cooking and washing dishes in restaurants, scrubbing floors in office buildings. Many worked in what was called in-service, meaning that they were employed as household help in wealthy homes, working there as maids, housekeepers, cooks, and kitchen help. Many new arrivals found work while waiting at Castle Garden for clearance to come ashore. The facility had an office where wealthy American families could choose servants from among the newly arrived young Irish women.

As soon as they were old enough to work, the children began to earn money to help their families. Young girls went to work in the sewing shops. Boys sold newspapers, swept the floors of saloons and stores, served as office boys or messengers for business concerns.

Their struggle to find work and survive was for decades made more difficult, and even dangerous, because of their religion—Roman Catholicism. The United States in the mid-1800s was a predominantly Protestant country, as it had been since the days before its founding. The flood of Catholics was greeted with a hostility that often exploded in violence—attacks on priests and nuns, and on churches and schools.

The American dislike and distrust of Roman Catholics stemmed mostly from the belief that Catholic businessmen, political leaders, and clergy were obedient mainly to their religious leaders in Rome rather than to the United States. The suspicion that Irish Catholics would not be completely loyal to their new nation persisted well into the twentieth century. In the presidential election of 1928, it was a fear that contributed to the defeat of Democratic candidate Alfred E. Smith, the first Catholic to seek the White House. (Other factors also contributed to Smith's defeat, among them his opposition to the Prohibition Amendment of 1919, which banned the sale of intoxicating liquor in the nation.) The United States had to wait until the presidential election of 1960 and the victory of John F. Kennedy to see the first Catholic enter the White House.

Irish women found that domestic service provided them with some of their greatest opportunities for employment—as maids, housekeepers, cooks, and child care "nannies" for prosperous families.

"No Irish Need Apply"

"No Irish Need Apply" was sung during the 1863 New York City Civil War draft riots, and remains popular among Irish Americans today. Interestingly enough, there is little or no evidence to support the fact that the slogan "No Irish Need Apply" ever appeared in print at all, or was posted in public places. Some say "No Irish Need Apply" was more of an urban legend than actual fact. The discrimination described in the song was probably attributed more to anti-Catholicism than to the Irish themselves.

The warning was set to music in the 1870s by Kathleen O'Neil, a popular singer of the day. The tune quickly became a comic favorite on the vaudeville stage.

I'm a decent lad just landed from the town of Ballyfad;

I want a situation and I want it very bad.

I've seen employment advertised. "It's just the thing," says I.

But the dirty spalpeen* ended with "No Irish Need Apply."

"Whoo," says I, "that is an insult, but to get the place I'll try."

So I went to see the blackguard with his "No Irish Need Apply."

* Rascal

Chorus:

Some do think it is a misfortune to be christened Pat or Dan,
But to me it is an honor to be born an Irishman.

I started out to find the house, I got there might soon;
I found the old chap seated—he was reading the Tribune.
I told him what I came for, when he in a rage did fly;
"No!" he says. "You are a Paddy, and no Irish need apply."
Then I gets my dander rising, and I'd like to black his eye
For to tell an Irish gentleman "No Irish Need Apply."

Repeat Chorus

I couldn't stand it longer so a-hold of him I took,
And I gave him such a welting as he'd get at Donnybrook.
And he hollered "Milia Murther," and to get away did try,
And swore he'd never write again "No Irish Need Apply."
Well, he made a big apology, I told him then goodbye.
Saying "When next you want a beating, write "No Irish Need Apply."

The famine finally came to an end in 1851, leaving behind a blasted Ireland, with more than a million of its people dead, and more than another million gone from its shores. But the end of the hunger did not signal the end of the migration to the United States and elsewhere. Once started, the movement could not be stopped.

John Kennedy Speaks on His Religion

In 1960, John F. Kennedy's bid for the presidency was endangered by the widespread suspicion that, once in the White House, he would be more loyal to the Roman Catholic Church than to his country. In a speech before a meeting of Protestant ministers in Houston, Texas, he stated his position on his religion and his loyalty to his nation:

Because I am a Catholic, and no Catholic has ever been elected President, the real issues in this campaign have been obscured. . . .

So it is apparently necessary for me to state once again, not what kind of church I believe in, for that should be important only to me, but what kind of America I believe in.

I believe in an America where the separation of church and state is absolute. . . .

I believe in a President whose views of religion are his own private affair. . . .

This is the kind of America I believe in—and this is the kind of America I fought for in the South Pacific and the kind my brother died for in Europe. No one suggested then that we might have a "divided loyalty," that we did "not believe in liberty" or that we belonged to a disloyal group that threatened "the freedoms for which our forefathers died."

The first and only Catholic to become president of the United States was John Fitzgerald Kennedy—but it was his religion, not his Irish background, that was held against him. Kennedy made it clear that religion would be no bar to his loyalty to the United States and he was elected to the office in 1960—but the religious loyalty of Protestant nominees for the office had never been questioned.

Contrary to common newspaper usage, I am not the Catholic candidate for President. I am the Democratic Party's candidate for President who happens to be a Catholic. I do not speak for my church on public matters . . . and the church does not speak for me. . . .

If this election is decided on the basis that 40 million Americans lost their chance of being President on the day they were baptized, then it is the whole nation that will be the loser in the eyes of Catholics and non-Catholics around the world, in the eyes of history, and in the eyes of our own people.

Passengers crowd the deck while others come down the ship's gangway on landing at Castle Garden in this photographic copy of a painting by Samuel Waugh.

Five

After the Famine

In 1851, six years after its arrival, the potato famine began to depart. But its passing did not mark the end of the Irish flight from home. Thousands went on booking passage to join the loved ones who had gone before them and to leave behind all the hardships and sorrows that they had borne for years. As reported, 1,167,000 people left Ireland during the famine years. Now, in the decades leading up to 1900, another 2.5 million would also leave. Between 1877 and 1879, many fled when the potato crop again failed and devastated large areas of the island's northwestern region. As usual, most sailed to the United States while others went elsewhere, chiefly to Canada, South America, South Africa, Australia, and New Zealand.

In total, these figures, when joined by the million or more famine deaths, came to more than 4.6 million people. This marked a loss of slightly more than 50 percent of the 8.2 million people tallied in the census of 1841. In a time when populations were increasing throughout the Western world, Ireland and Norway were the only European nations to show major declines.

The Post-Famine Years in Ireland

THE NEXT YEARS WERE MARKED BY TWO STRUGGLES THAT BROUGHT significant changes to life in Ireland. First, the financial sufferings that the country's tenant farmers had endured during the years of want—principally, the loss of their homes through eviction—led to the passage in the mid-1880s of a law safeguarding their property rights. It contained provisions for fair rent charges, protection of renters against illegal evictions, and government loans for those who wished to purchase land for farming.

The second change began to take shape long before the famine and would not come to fruition until early in the twentieth century. The change stemmed from the widespread anger that had erupted in 1801 when the British government ended Irish political activities by abolishing the Irish Parliament and decreeing that its members must now sit in the British Parliament.

That move, ending the last vestiges of independent political activity by their representatives, both infuriated and frustrated the Irish people. They wanted to see matters corrected, but were sharply divided into two camps over how to get the job done. One camp wanted complete independence from Britain. The other urged what was called home rule, meaning that the Irish would be allowed to govern themselves but would remain a part of the British Empire.

The struggle over the future course of the country raged through the last decades of the nineteenth century and into the twentieth century. Home Rule was approved by Parliament in 1914, but was suspended due to World War I. Then came a period marked by guerrilla warfare against

*Evictions from their cottages was a common sight when families were unable to pay their rents.
Often, those evicted were left stranded by the roadside, with their few possessions piled around
them.*

the British authorities and by angry disagreements between the nation's Protestant and Catholic populations, with neither eager for a government that would be led by or shared with the other. Finally, on December 6, 1921, after long negotiations between Irish and British representatives, the country won a new status and a new name—the Irish Free State.

Of Ireland's thirty-two counties, the Free State was composed of twenty-six, all of which were located in the southern half of the island and chiefly populated by Catholics. The remaining six—Fermanagh, Armagh, Down, Antrim, Londonderry, and Tyrone—lay to the north and were allowed to remain out of the state because of their Protestant faith and their long-standing loyalty to the British Crown. The new state was given dominion status, making it virtually an independent country. In 1937, it was renamed Eire and became a republic, but remained within the British Commonwealth of Nations. In 1949, Eire left the Commonwealth and was renamed the Republic of Ireland.

The Thousands Who Traveled

THE THOUSANDS WHO TRAVELED TO NORTH AMERICA DURING AND AFTER the famine struggled with decades of challenge—the challenge of venturing into an unknown land and finding success in the many fields of endeavor that it offered.

Actually, it was a new chapter in the challenge for the Irish in the United States, whose history dates back to the 1600s when the first Irish arrived in the British colonies as indentured servants (penniless people who bound themselves to work for others for a specific period in exchange for the passage money across the Atlantic). The challenge continued in the 1700s when Irish rebels and convicted criminals were transported to the colonies as punishment. Many descendants of these and other early arrivals fought on the colonial side in the Revolutionary War.

The American struggle for freedom from Britain gave the infant

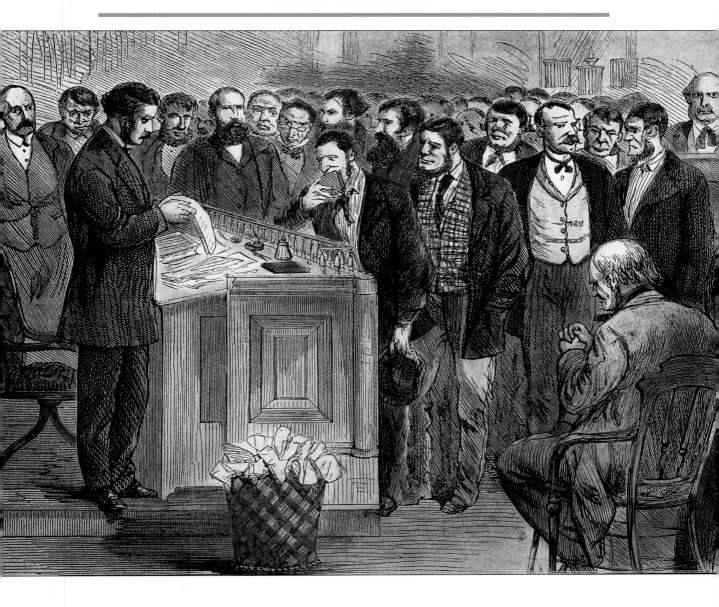

Many newcomers quickly took steps to become U.S. citizens. Here, a group is being examined by a judge before being sworn in as naturalized citizens.

country one of its first national heroes of Irish descent—Charles Carroll of Carrollton, Maryland. A member of a large clan that had begun arriving in the New World in 1688, Carroll became the only Catholic to sign the Declaration of Independence. He later helped to formulate Maryland's state constitution and, from 1789 to 1792, represented his state in the U.S. Senate.

Quite as important in early American history was Charles's cousin, John Carroll, who, in 1790, was appointed America's first Catholic bishop. A year earlier, he set aside a section of his family's estate as the site for a school that would eventually become Georgetown University.

While most of the Irish who arrived in the United States during and after the famine settled close to where they had first come ashore, thousands did venture forth and, in time, settled throughout the country. In 1848, while the famine was still raging, Irish newcomers were among the hordes that traveled west to the California goldfields. A dozen years later, the ranks of both the Union and Confederate armies were manned with Irish troops. Then, in the wake of the Civil War, the Irish were among the various nationalities that laid the tracks for the nation's burgeoning railroad systems.

By the dawn of the twentieth century, the Irish were solidly planted in their new homeland, represented in every field of endeavor. Just how diverse and valuable were their achievements for the country can be seen in the brief stories of just a few of their most distinguished members:

John Barry (1745–1803)—An Irish-born seaman, Barry became a naval officer in the Revolutionary War. Because of his successful training programs, he is often credited with being the "Father of the United States Navy."

John McCormick (1809–1884)—Son of Scotch-Irish immigrants, John McCormick revolutionized farming with his McCormick reaper. Before

Born in Ireland, Archbishop John Joseph Hughes of New York City worked to further Catholic education and health care. He was one of the founders of Fordham University (known in his lifetime as St. John's College). It was during his years as New York's archbishop that St. Patrick's Cathedral was built.

its development, a man could cut only two or three acres of grain per day. With the reaper, the daily total could be increased to twenty acres.

Henry Ford (1863–1947)—Son of immigrants, Ford revolutionized the infant automotive industry.

Nellie Bly (1864–1922)—Daughter of parents whose forebears came from Ireland in the early 1800s, Bly won international fame as a journalist.

*Among the more illustrious descendants of
Irish emigrants to the United States have
been Henry Ford, who revolutionized the
automobile industry in its early days, and
Nellie Bly, whose investigative reporting
long predated that of Woodward and
Bernstein of* All the President's Men *fame.*

Anne Sullivan Macy (1866–1936)—A woman of impaired sight and the daughter of immigrants from County Limerick, Anne Sullivan Macy is revered as the tutor who taught blind, deaf, and mute Helen Keller how to communicate with the outside world. Keller went on to a life of work on behalf of the handicapped.

Father Edward Flanagan (1886–1948)—Born, educated, and ordained a Catholic priest in Ireland, Father Flanagan opened a Nebraska shelter for homeless boys in 1917. It proved a great success, was christened Boys Town in 1922, won international fame, and was expanded to take in young women in 1979.

Eugene O'Neill (1888–1953)—The son of immigrant parents, O'Neill won national and international fame as a dramatist. His finest plays included *The Emperor Jones, Mourning Becomes Electra*, and *Long Day's Journey Into Night*. He was awarded four Pulitzer Prizes and, in 1936, the Nobel Prize for Literature. His father was James O'Neill, a poor immigrant who won fame as an actor of the American stage.

Throughout their years in the United States, citizens of Irish descent have shown a marked talent for political activity. Whether Catholic or Protestant, they have served at all levels of government—local, state, national, and international. Of the country's forty-three presidents, at least nine have come from Irish backgrounds. Beginning with earliest of their number to serve in the White House, they are listed here:

Andrew Jackson	(1767–1845)	7th president
James K. Polk	(1795–1849)	11th
Ulysses S. Grant	(1822–1885)	18th
Chester A. Arthur	(1829–1886)	21st
Grover Cleveland	(1839–1908)	22nd and 24th

William McKinley	(1843–1901)	25th
Woodrow Wilson	(1856–1924)	28th
John F. Kennedy	(1917–1963)	35th
Ronald Reagan	(1911–)	40th

In choosing to make the United States their new home, millions of Irish men, women, and children chose a path that has been followed through the years by all the people who have come here in search of new lives, new beginnings. These people include the earliest European settlers, the Africans who were first brought here in bondage, the Jews who came from all over the world, the Chinese who were early banned unjustly from entering the country, and many others. They all have patiently built lives for themselves and their descendants. In the process, they have fashioned one of the most unique and varied cultures ever seen in the world. The process that they began continues to this day.

Bibliography

Boyer, Paul S., ed. *The Oxford Companion to United States History*. New York: Oxford University Press, 2001.

Carnes, Mark C., John A. Garraty, and Patrick Williams. *Mapping America's Past: A Historical Atlas*. New York: Henry Holt, 1996.

Coffey, Michael, ed., with text by Terry Golway. *The Irish in America*. New York: Hyperion, 1997.

Costigan, Giovanni. *A History of Modern Ireland, with a Sketch of Earlier Times*. New York: Pegasus, 1969.

Cronin, Mike. *A History of Ireland*. New York and Hampshire, England: Palgrave Publications, 2001.

Eiseman, Alberta. *From Many Lands*. New York: Atheneum, 1970.

Evans, Harold, with Gail Buckland and Kevin Baker. *The American Century*. New York: Alfred A. Knopf, 1998.

Gray, Peter. *The Irish Famine*. New York: Harry N. Abrams, 1995.

Hoobler, Dorothy and Thomas. *The Irish American Family Album*. New York: Oxford University Press, 1995.

Keneally, Thomas. *The Great Shame: and the Triumph of the Irish in the English-Speaking World*. London: Serpentine Publishing, 1998.

Laxton, Edward. *The Famine Ships: The Irish Exodus to America*. New York: Henry Holt, 1998.

Llewelyn, Morgan. *The Essential Library for Irish Americans*. New York: Tom Doherty Associates, 2000.

Melville, Herman. *Redburn: His First Voyage*. Evanston and Chicago, Illinois: Northwestern University Press and Newberry Library, 1969.

Miller, Kerby A. *Emigrants and Exiles: Ireland and the Irish Exodus to North America*. New York: Oxford University Press, 1985.

Miller, Kerby A., and Paul Wagner. *Out of Ireland: The Story of Irish Emigration to America*. Lanham, MD: Madison Books, 2001.

Philbin, Tom. *The Irish 100: A Ranking of the Most Influent Irish of All Time*. Kansas City, MO: Andrews McMeel, 1999.

Poirteir, Cathal, ed. *The Great Irish Famine*. Dublin, Ireland: Mercier Press, 1995.

Tripp, Eleanor B. *To America: The Story of Why People Left Their Homes for the New Land*. New York: Harcourt, Brave & World, 1969.

Further Reading

Corbishley, Mike, et al. *The Young Oxford History of Britain & Ireland*. New York: Oxford University Press, 1997.

Fitzpatrick, Marie-Louise. *The Long March: The Choctaw's Gift to Irish Famine Relief*. Philadelphia: Tricycle Press, 1999.

Watts, James F. *The Irish Americans*. New York: Chelsea House, 1995.

Index